Motherhood on the Line

Sorting Out What Influences Your Day

Holly M. Giles

Copyright © 2019 Holly M. Giles

All rights reserved. No part of this publication may be reproduced, stored in a retrieval system, or transmitted in any form or by any means – electronic, mechanical, digital, photocopy, recording, or any other – except for brief quotations in printed reviews, without the prior permission of Holly M. Giles

Cover design: Megan Jurvis Designs

ISBN 978-0-9992907-3-6

Dedication

To my boys, Grayson and Grant, for bringing your father and I along on adventures we could have never imagined. To my husband Curtis, thank you for holding steady through it all and loving me always. And to my mom, thank you for encouraging my big dreams, and always having what I need at the General Store.

CONTENTS

	Prologue	1
1	The Beginning of the Line	9
2	The Lie Homemakers Tell	17
3	Her Life is Better Than Mine	31
4	Unwrap your Gifts	39
5	The Utopian Society Effect	45
6	Friendships at the Clothesline	51
7	Where Did All the Cookies Go?	65
8	Wash, Dry, Fold and Repeat	73
9	A Marriage Hung Out to Dry	77
10	The Caretaker of the Clothespins	83
11	The Beauty Within the Clothesline	87
12	Fear in the Hole	93

Prologue

It had been four weeks since hurricane Irma, and life still felt disorganized. Our yard was littered with debris, and even the grocery stores had not caught up with simple food like eggs and milk. The kicker was the coffee creamer. Every store was out of coffee creamer of every kind. Why? Don't they know we are recovering from a disaster? Don't take away our coffee too! Anyway, I felt like life was out of control again, and I didn't know what to tackle first.

My son's Grayson and Grant's school lessons were haphazardly done in between working on tree clearing jobs with my husband Curtis. The laundry was literally multiplying before my eyes and had now taken over, not only the couch, but the foot of our bed and locating socks was becoming impossible. The vacuum cleaner gave out the day after our power was restored from the storm. You may not think that is a big deal, however after eight days with no electricity and living with boys who are working tree jobs and bringing in dirt and debris on their shoes, and I was looking forward to vacuuming the entire house, twice. I was now down to using only the broom, electric sweeper, and microfiber cloths to clean the rug and tile, and to look the other way when leaves blew in the front door.

Washing clothes had become a test of strength for my nose. Our water smelled like rotten eggs, and so did the air outside. We live on a small lake, near several significant waterways that were severely impacted by the hurricane. The impact caused such a foul stench each morning that you needed a strong stomach to take in the odor.

Once the power had been restored, I hoped I could gather myself together to find normal again. Whatever that looked like now.

Historically, I have been a strong person who could weather these situations with grace. Pulling up my bootstraps and moving forward is my motto that at forty-eight had served me well so far. Yet, my bootstraps were broke this time. This time I felt the mountain I had been climbing all these years, just had a mudslide. Being a good mother, teaching my boys at home, creating the home environment I always wanted, and believed I hadn't achieved yet, was now turning to rubble. I was sliding back and losing ground. I was back to square one, lost.

In the weeks after the hurricane, I felt ashamed of how poorly I had dealt with the situation. The truth was I was not in control anymore. My schedule was in disarray, all activities had been canceled for the foreseeable future, and all I could do was take one day at a time. I could only accomplish what needed to be done THAT day the best I could do. Honestly, it wasn't my best at all. Each day was a difficult task to put food on the table for my family and get everyone to move towards normal.

Then one afternoon, I headed to the kitchen with purpose. I was going to pull together some concoction of a meal from the chaos. A little of this, a bit of that, and call it supper. However, an odd smell preceded me as I walked toward the kitchen.

When I rounded the corner, I found Grant, eleven, had taken over all the counter space with his fishing lure project. Grant is an avid fisherman and visionary. By visionary, I mean he sees grand opportunities in whatever his pursuits are, and he usually has to build or make something from these ideas of his. This time, he discovered that he could melt down his used plastic lures and make new ones. Now, as you read this, it sounds incredible, right? Yes, a child who explores possibilities and gets to take action!

Let me set the scene for you. Making your own lures requires constructing a mold. Grant's chosen medium was

Plaster of Paris. He mixed the plaster in one of my lovely melamine bowls. Next, he needed to melt the gummy style plastic lures with unknown ingredients in my glass batter bowl in the microwave (odd smell). Then, he poured the hot melted plastic into his mold with my good silverware.

So, as I round the corner in the kitchen and take in what has transpired since I was on a few business calls, my anger and irritability reached a palatable level. Dried plaster was on the counter, the stove top, and on the floor. It was on the utensils in the utensil holder, and all on one side of my utensil holder. I adore my utensil holder. It is made from three black, metal cheese graters that are turned upside down and attached to a spindle. I bought it last year on a clearance splurge at Cracker Barrel. Do you know how many tiny, little holes and crevices in a cheese grater that plaster can get stuck?

I moved closer to survey the damage and just as I was about to let Grant know how I felt about this mess, in walks Grayson, fourteen, with the food dehydrator. He announces that everyone must clear the kitchen so he can make "the best jerky ever!". I had already forgotten about the four pounds of ground venison that had been curing in my refrigerator for the last twenty-four hours.

I shook my head and began talking to myself under my breath about tiny kitchens, disrespectful boys, how my life ended up like this, and why I felt like I was always camping INSIDE my house. I wanted normal. Why can't we have one day where school lessons are fully completed, the floor stayed clean for more than thirty seconds, and nothing got broken or destroyed? Normal like other families.

My face was getting hotter by the second. I was just about to hurl my accusations onto the boys when Grant squealed with excitement.

"Momma, I did it, I made a lure!" he says, "Momma, will you watch me make another one?"

As I looked into that sweet boy's face and saw the twinkling in those sky blue eyes, my heart melted, I took a long, deep breath and said, "Of course, I would love to."

After the smell of burnt plastic had dissipated from the microwave, I went back to fixing supper. Grayson was busy at the island with his jerky gun placing his Slim Jim style jerky sticks on the trays of the dehydrator. Grant was mixing up plaster for a new mold and different style lure. This time he was using disposable bowls and utensils. Here we were, crammed in the kitchen, each doing something completely different, yet sharing in the experience together.

I stopped mixing up the burgers for supper and turned around, and watched them. I soaked in the moment of my boys who I had been pouring my days into, molding, shaping and pruning at the feet of Jesus for the last fourteen years and realized what a fool I had been. What I have been aspiring to and searching for on that mountain, was right here. I was living the life I always wanted, yet lived in fear that I would never achieve it.

Grayson and Grant were following their passions, living them out with action because Curtis and I have given them time to do so, AND they were sharing it with me, their mother. These days disguised as chaos are actually the best days of my life. When I choose to let society's barometer gauge how I look at the success of my family, I will always come unraveled at the seams. Let's face it, we are not typical, but who is?

However, if I would take the time to look beyond what I believe is dis-order, I would see the best that being a mom has to offer. I would see the true blessings, and the "perfect" family is right here among the plaster, fishing lures, and the spicy jerky.

This story is for you. It is for me and all of us trying to find meaning in our life, love, and happiness among the chaos. Grab your cup of coffee or sweet tea and join me on my back porch as we share a few stories.

Curtis and I have chosen to educate our children at home. We always have, even to the delight and dismay of family and friends. Whether you do as well or not, doesn't preclude you from getting the most out of this book. I speak of it throughout because it is woven into our lives, but if you are married and have children, you can glean from these chapters.

Chapter One

The Beginning of the Line

Life is a series of stories that we share. Storytelling has been the foundation of humankind since the beginning. Family honor, education, warnings of danger, and even directions have been told through story, either spoken, drawn, or written.

I fell in love with stories as a little girl. My grandfather read aloud to my grandmother every night. On my weekend visits, I could partake in stories of the world that he read in a voice that made those stories come alive.

I am now a storyteller in my own right. I tell stories of hope, failure, and inspiration to families about life, love, children, and dirty dishes. I am just sixteen years into this season of being a mother and twenty-five years as a wife. I share this particular life adventure with you, at this time, as a reminder to always keep moving forward in finding the balance in life. Although my journey is far from over, I hope God has shown me that we need hope, encouragement, and even a lifeline along the way. First, let me share the condensed version of how I came to find myself lost and just trying to survive with two young children in tow.

Curtis and I married at the ages of twenty-three and twenty-four. We had visions of sugar plums and fairy tales dancing in our heads, well at least mine. The next years to come would be nothing like happily ever after. In our way, we would have to come to grips with reality and discover what holding on for better or worse truly meant.

On our first night home after our honeymoon, Curtis vomited all night from food poisoning. I wasn't quite sure what to do for him, but I was a little miffed that he chose to vomit in our brand new mauve-colored bathroom trash can we received as a wedding gift. The next morning he asked me to call his mother because she would know what to do. I was mad at first because Curtis wouldn't let me help him, but then I called her because I honestly didn't know what to do and thought we needed her to make it through this crisis. I still have that mauve trash can after twenty-five years, and yes, I think of that day every time I empty it.

At the end of that first week at home as newlyweds, after the poisoning incident, I cooked our first meal as a couple. I was so proud that I pulled off that all-in-one packet of red beans and rice that I was beaming. No compliments were given, but a few negative ones were, and I ended up locking myself in the bathroom, crying. I was certain we had made a terrible mistake. Oh boy, did I have a lot to learn?

In the first six years of our marriage, we lost six significant family members. Grandparents that had raised us shaped us and been our best friends. Uncles and cousins too. Some expected, several unexpected, and a few with lingering issues that slowly took their lives in painful ways.

It was difficult to understand how to help each other through the grieving and loss. Time began to pass by, and my dream of having children was slipping away too. I always wanted to be a mother. Deep down, it is all I ever wanted to be. Once the fog began to lift, Curtis and I realized there might be a reason why we had not been blessed with a child yet. Tests revealed I would not be able to have children without intervention — the next four years filled with treatments, shots, and insemination. The stress of all the pressure fractured our marriage.

The Beginning of the Line

In the eighth year of our marriage, I became depressed. My relationship with Jesus was mediocre at best, as well as my husband. I contemplated walking away from my life with Curtis and starting over. After a few failed attempts, which I am not sure he was aware of, I decided maybe I was looking in the wrong direction. I fell to my knees and asked for God's forgiveness. I had become consumed with becoming a mother and living the life I had dreamed up in my head, that I was not seeking the truth He had for me. Curtis and I began mending our marriage. Together we had to accept that we may not have children.

A few months passed, and our relationship had taken a turn for the better. I was walking with Jesus daily and was hopeful about the future. Then, I became pregnant with the miracle baby our doctors said was not possible.

Grayson Walter Giles was born right on time in February. He cried for seventeen hours a day for eight months. I fell deep into what I now know was postpartum depression. Lack of sleep and a baby who would not stop crying took our lives in another direction.

We visited the doctor frequently with various symptoms that went un-diagnosed until he was three years old. A brain

MRI revealed he had had a stroke, possibly in utero or at birth. This news was so unreal it literally silenced us as a family and overshadowed the joy of our new baby at home, Grant Henry.

The next seven years were spent getting help for Grayson. Physical therapy, speech therapy, occupational therapy, tests, more MRI's, sleep studies, and neurology appointments. We ignored the fact that this was crippling us financially, and Curtis' job was in trouble. Our son needed help. We had to do whatever we needed for him to recover. We also wanted to put blinders on to the possibility that Grant had Tourette's Syndrome and had begun showing verbal and physical tics early in his life.

Now that I have your attention, I did say the condensed version. There is more to our story of hope and healing with a special needs child. But that is for another time. What I want you to know now is that Grayson is sixteen, and Grant is thirteen at the time of this writing. They are magnificent and doing wonderfully in their lives.

My life has not gone according to my plan at all. God has been throwing me curve balls for years now in preparation for this, being the wife and mother he has called me to be. I have found a way to grow into being a wife, mother, and home educator through faith in God's plan, some incredible wisdom from my grandmother, and plenty of mistakes along the way.

In the following chapters, I get real with you about issues I believe keep us from truly experiencing the life God has for us. I will focus on simple tools for homemaking, home educating, parenting, marriage, and womanhood.

I am not an expert at anything, and I am still growing as the seasons' change in my life. I hope that through my story, you can become inspired to thrive with your family in the different seasons that come with being a wife and raising children.

Moving Forward

Let's jump right in with some questions that will set the tone for the book. I believe that writing down the answers will give you a reference point as we move forward. I know you just want to read this, grab your golden nuggets, and move on. I have been there, and I get it. However, I have discovered that writing it down, highlighting it, re-reading it, seeing it and dealing with it, whatever IT is for you, can propel you forward. Forward is where we want to go, isn't it?

The days will pass, weeks and then years, we can't stop it so we might as well clean the mud off our rubber boots right now. So we don't get stuck along the way.

Here are the questions to ponder and answer as you read this book. Tweak the item to fit your situation, but answer them truthfully.

In truth, we find freedom.

- Do you have multiple children under the age of four?
- Are you juggling multiple age groups in your parenting or homeschooling?
- Have you doubted your ability to keep up with your kids activities, schoolwork, be a wife, be a mother, keep your home going, *and* keep your sanity?
- Do you feel lonely in this season of your life?
- Have you found it hard to make friends as a mom or homeschooling mom?
- Are you having difficulty with marital issues?
- Do you have issues from your past that have been buried but possibly affecting your life now?

I have answered yes to all of these questions at one time or another. I think we all do. The problem is, how do we handle it and come out better on the other side. Together, we will address some simple tools and ideas that you can put into place right now.

Having a few tools in your back pocket can make the difference from making it through a stressful day or hiding in the bathroom with chocolate and crying for the afternoon. Yes, I have done that too. However, when I come out, the kids and the problems are still there. I began to realize that finding a way to deal with these stresses was a much better plan because I was doing it so often that my pants were getting too tight from all the chocolate bars and brownies. As I did, they began to happen fewer and farther apart.

Chapter Two
The Lie Homemakers Tell

My grandmother, Mona (Meemee), was an amazing woman. She raised four boys, each a year apart, kept a spotless home, I mean on the floor scrubbing and ironing bed sheets spotless. She cooked piles of the best southern food you could soak your cornbread in, the sweet tea pitcher was never empty, and people were always showing up at her home for a visit. As a little girl, I watched all of this through rose-colored glasses and wanted to be just like her.

I spent my childhood sitting on the stool next to her stove, watching her chop, mix, and bake. She had family recipes that were a staple such as field peas and cornbread. Her tomato sandwiches on oatmeal bread were delicious. But her buttermilk pie, that was worth the wait for each holiday. Meemee never actually taught me how to make any of it. I just soaked the process into my memories.

Bleach was her number one cleaning tool, and her

tablecloths were always crisp and ironed. Laundry was going daily, even though all her children were grown. Although, my grandfather could make enough messes for several children put together! Meemee was always busy doing something with her hands.

Most days that I was visiting, friends and family would randomly pull up in their backyard driveway and sit awhile in the swing. Conversations were always full of laughter, memories, and the future of this country. I was a shy child, so I would listen from a tree branch or on the swing next to my grandmother. There were always plenty of mason jars full of tea (because re-using the jars was frugal, not in style) and a sweet treat to share with the unexpected company.

I delighted in that sense of community. Friends near and far, always feeling at home in my grandparent's backyard. They had a shared history with so many people. The people who came were neighbors whose children grew up with theirs, co-workers of my grandfather, who were a part of the camping and fishing days, or church members. No one was ever a stranger, and no one ever left empty-handed.

When I grew up and got married, I envisioned cooking, cleaning, and entertaining like my grandmother. It didn't look hard. The reality was I honestly didn't know how to cook anything or get the right ratio of water to bleach without some damage. I grew up as an only child in a single parent household (mother) so sharing a closet and a bathroom with a man was a rude awakening.

After a brief stint of ruining anything possible with cleaners and setting off smoke alarms, I finally realized I was not able to clean to the standards of Mona. I did not think it was possible. Somehow her impeccable skills had not rubbed off on me. Curtis confessed in later years how he sneaked off many nights to grab something to eat at Arby's after one of my not-so-great suppers. I had to work hard for several years to accomplish both skills. I finally began to love cooking and trying new recipes.

When children came into our lives, the chores began to feel like I was always on a hamster wheel. Just when I thought I had finished one thing, another needed desperate attention. Diapers, dishes, and dog hair got the better of me. The laundry started to become this overwhelming task that never seemed to be complete. Do you ever feel like that? With our first child, I realized how clean our house wasn't and was frantic with him to not getting dirty or near the dogs. Our second child was lucky if he was wearing clean clothes, and the dog usually found the pacifier first.

As my boys got older, the messes seemed to get bigger instead of smaller. Both of them are outdoor kids. They spend most of their days getting dirty, fishing in the lake, playing in the woods, and making my floors muddy. For years I have been telling people that we live a camping lifestyle. Yes, I tend to get strange looks in return as they wait for the punch line. But in the early years, what I wanted to say is I felt like I was living in a house full of savages, and I am on the edge of insanity. I felt like I was being closed in by the upkeep of the house. The monotony of my days was strangling me, and I stayed frustrated with everyone.

Mona had moved to another state before my children were born. I missed having her close to give me advice. We spoke by phone frequently, and we took the boys to see her as much as we could. On one of our visits, I reluctantly shared with her my inability to do it all as a mother. I felt that I was not equipped to handle all that raising children entailed. I wasn't good enough. Cleaning was not my favorite thing to do, and I felt like I was missing precious time with these boys. I did not want to look like a failure in her eyes because I believed she was the perfect mom and did it all without complaint.

Mona was about eighty-eight at that visit. She had begun to lose her eyesight and was not able to get around very well. She spent most of her days reflecting on her life. I was expecting a few harsh words from her about my attitude toward my never-ending chore list. However, what she said instead rings through my mind still today.

She said," Holly, when I was raising my children, I could never keep up with the housework. I worked tirelessly every day to keep that house spotless. I thought that was what I was supposed to do. I was raised in a time where you were judged by the cleanliness of your home and care of your family. Sometimes I would look out the window and see other mothers pushing their babies down the sidewalk in a buggy, and I would weep. I did not understand how they could get all their chores, cooking, and housework done and have any time left to play with their babies. It is my biggest regret. Please, let the floors be dirty Holly if it means time with your husband and your children. If I had only realized that early on, I might have a different story to tell."

Wow. As Meemee told me that story, tears ran down my face. I felt so sad for the young Mona who had missed out on so much with her children. Little things that make up the unique places in your heart. Things a mother cherishes. I realized I did not want to have that regret.

Let's take a look at homemaking in your home and see what you can let go of in the season you are in today. I am not a type-A personality with organizational charts and spreadsheets for you. My thoughts are strictly for survival. I began to think about what is the most important things that need to be cleaned to not succumb to filth. It may look different each season, depending on the age of the children in my home. How could I keep daily living afloat and make the most of my time with the boys? It boils down to three specific questions:

- If you could do nothing else, what is the absolute ONE thing that needs to be done each day for you to survive?

The answer will look different for every person. Think about the season you are in, the ages of your children, and where the most significant source of frustration is for you. If you had to let go of everything for a week, what one task would help you make it through?

For me, it is sweeping the floors. Piles of dirt and leaves are continually coming in the back door. It can make me cringe and feel like I will lose my mind. I do not like the sound or feel of crunching under my feet on the tile floors. If I can keep the floors swept, I can survive.

- Is that a job that has to be done by you, or could your spouse or one of your children do it?

I know you type-A mamas are cringing right now, but let's get serious. If we are talking about survival mode for those seasons where you need it, can someone else do that job for you?

Grant, my youngest, is the floor sweeper. That poor child sweeps floors several times a day. He knows I start getting a twitch in my eye when dog hair and dirt start rolling around invisible piles. He has an electric sweeper that is entertaining to him, and he has to break out a real broom too by the end of the day. His work has yet to pass a white glove test, but it is good enough to keep me from getting the hibby-jibbies (southern slang for anxiety).

- What is the one thing you can do that would make your spouse happy each day /week when he comes home?

This is a loaded question that may receive some grumbles from a stressed-out mamma but bear with me. I was at a workshop on cleaning and organization recently, yes it is a constant battle for me, and the speaker asked us that question. It was like a light bulb moment. During her presentation, she told us that when she asked her husband this question after sixteen years of marriage, she was at a breaking point. She had four young kids and was consumed with what needed to be accomplished in a day. Her husband's answer was that he would absolutely love his work shirts ironed. He didn't care about toys on the floor or dishes in the sink, but it would make him happy to have ironed shirts.

As the speaker told her story, I realized that we put so much pressure on ourselves to live up to a standard we set for ourselves that is unrealistic. It boils down to communication. I know I did not come up with some undiscovered solution that is going to change households across America, but no matter how long you have been married, it is true. Communication is the number one struggle aside from money in marriages today.

Assumptions can be easier to deal with than a heart to heart conversation. Unspoken actions by a spouse can inadvertently become ques by which we base our reactions. It is a slippery slope that can start as a pebble and end up a boulder by the time it reaches the bottom. We have had a few boulders lying around our home over the years.

He said, she said, so I thought?

We forget to communicate, and we begin to assume. We assume so many things because we are so busy changing diapers, cooking dinner, and figuring out a math problem with a teenager, that the thought to have a real and meaningful conversation with our spouse is delusional.

It is much easier to begin harboring thoughts about what our spouse thinks and churn it in our minds for years until it becomes a reality. I know I am not the only woman who believes her husband is blind, deaf, and mute when it comes to household issues. I am famous for conjuring up all kinds of reasons why my husband does not race in the back door every day and start a load of laundry, finish the dishes in the sink, set out dinner for the kids and whisk me off to the bedroom and tell me I am the most beautiful woman in the world.

My truth is cooking dinner every day festers in me like a tick in a dog's ear on occasion. Why the people in my house have to eat three meals a day is beyond my comprehension. Right now, I have two teenagers that can obliterate two hundred dollars worth of food in thirty-six hours and not leave a crumb behind.

I pondered my theory about communication after that workshop, and then, my boulder about dinner blew up. Curtis came home from work, and it had been a rough day of lessons, errands, and ridiculously long wait time on the phone with the phone company. Dinner was not on my radar. The savages had raided the remains of our food supply at lunch, and there was not even enough to make a refrigerator casserole. In case you haven't made that meal, it is basically dumping all leftovers and random vegetables in a casserole dish, topping it with a can of soup and cheese and baking at 350 degrees for 30 minutes.

I apologized to Curtis about the barren kitchen and told him I had absolutely no idea what we were going to eat. I may have become teary-eyed. He looked at me and casually said "I don't expect you to cook every day, I don't cook at all, so I don't expect you to be responsible for my food all the time. We can figure it out." I believe I stood there looking at him dumbfounded for ten minutes. Like he had been speaking in an accent, and I was trying to piece together his words. I was stunned by his answer.

Over the last twenty-five years, I had been carrying this boulder that assumed he expected a hot meal on the table every day. I never asked if he expected that, I just assumed it was my duty to provide a good meal daily for my husband. Even if it was so unpalatable, he needed to sneak out for nourishment later.

I never actually asked him what he thought about it or if

it was important to him. I felt guilty and felt a twinge of resentment from him when I didn't cook. The reality was he wasn't feeling resentment towards me at all. He was thinking which fast food joint he was going to slip off to for a quick bite when there wasn't food at home or if there was still a stash of Little Debbie's in the hall closet.

I have heard this from moms on more than one occasion. I believe it may be universal. When a spouse is out of town or not coming home for dinner, mama doesn't cook. She and the kids forage in the refrigerator or even have cereal for supper. Do we have an ingrained assumption that we must cook dinner every night?

Communicate about meals. Put this idea into practice during your busiest seasons and let go of unrealistic expectations. Your husband may love to try his hand at a simple supper. Maybe he likes to grill, and can show off his talents once a week. Although my husband is allergic to the kitchen, he will happily fetch food from anywhere he can find it when I ask him to. Also, cooking two of the same meals at once and freezing the second in less busy times has saved our suppers many nights. There are a plethora of solutions out there. Find what works for you. Guess what? It is OK if your kids eat cereal for dinner.

The book of Ephesians speaks to us about marriage beginning in chapter five. Paul explains that we are to be imitators of God and walk in love. Harboring assumptions about our spouse prevents us from imitating God's love. Assumptions change our perspective of how we view our spouse and vice versa. Walking in wisdom calls us to be wise and submit to one another in fear of God. He also talks about the submission of wives and husbands to each other. This idea likewise applies to our communication with each other about our daily needs. It is easy to run off in the ditch here, which leads to ruts that get bigger over time.

→ What are some of the assumptions you have made in your marriage?

→ What are some of the assumptions your spouse has made about you?

Make a list of the ones you need to address in order of importance. Set aside time to speak with your spouse.

- Ask for forgiveness from each other.

- Make time to communicate.

- Hide a box of cereal and Little Debbie's for emergency situations.

Chapter Three

Her Life is Better Than Mine

Comparison is the death of joy – Mark Twain.

Don't compare yourself to the mom next door. How often do we hear those words? It is a universal mantra for women. Yet, we still do it. You know you do. How do I know? I do it too. When we are at a place where we aren't quite sure where we fit, it is easy to make assumptions about that mom who has it all together at playgroup. We can certainly put on a show and attempt to have it all together. However, that only hides the truth and lack of understanding of what is going on in our own life.

A touch of jealousy about a friend who appears to have the perfect house, kids, and husband can put us in a bad mood, and let's face it, turn on our own young. Sounds harsh but listen, I had dreams of my life turning out to be like an

American version of the Von Trapp family right down to the matching clothes. I have had my share of jealous rants because several other moms at co-op seemed to have that life, and I don't. I see them with their clean children in matching polo shirts. They play soccer, piano, violin, and travel with an orchestra. I hear about the equestrian events and Lego robotics competitions and all the photos on social media.

Meanwhile, I have one kid who takes my good silverware to play spoons in the backyard and the other blows incessantly into a six-foot-long PVC pipe, to the delight of our neighbors, and the only thing they will wear that matches is mud. By the way, do you have the problem of missing spoons? We are down to four from our wedding set since having children.

Comparison steals the joy in our own life

Comparing each others' lives is similar to the assumptions in our marriage. We can be entirely off base with our thinking. We may do out-of-the-ordinary things to make others believe we are just like them or try and hide our pain. Cute leggings and the latest diaper bag or tote can disguise loneliness, hurt, and exhaustion for a little while. But sooner or later, the elastic gives out, and something smelly leaks out of your pretty purse.

My favorite workshop that I present as a motivational speaker is where I tell people that my boys don't know the days of the week in order and are never quite sure what month it is. I get so many hugs from moms who are ashamed to tell people that about their children. You know you do it too. In a group of high achievers, you nod and smile, but are secretly worried your kids won't make it in the real world. It's true. I know it because of the hundreds of women who have told me so, and I think it about my boys on a weekly basis. The truth sets you free to feel those worries and find others who think it too.

Pain gussied up like a cowgirl

Grayson was turning five, and Grant was turning two. We were over a year into therapies and helping Grayson recover from his stroke. Our finances were stretched paper-thin, and loneliness had set in. We had been out of touch with many of our friends, and pretty much out of touch with life. For everyone else, life had gone on after Grayson's diagnosis. Most had bigger houses, better jobs, coffee meet-ups, and mommy and me classes. Curtis and I were still in our little house with no photos on the walls trying to make it day by day.

My hobbies used to be turning yard sale finds into cool stuff. But my years were too busy to enjoy doing any of those things anymore. Family parties and backyard gatherings were my specialties in years past. I loved to plan events down to every last detail. Those days were long forgotten.

Celebrating the boys' birthday seemed like a welcomed retreat, and I decided to go all in. It was time to see old friends and dust off the decorator in me. Their birthdays were only four days apart, so we usually celebrate them together. The boys chose a cowboy theme, and I ran with it. Yes, indeed, I could pull off an event to show just how good we were getting along. I made a life-size tee-pee out of bamboo, I directed my husband to make a "bull" out of saw horses for roping, and I hunted down a three-foot-tall stuffed horse for them to "ride." I planned an Indian beading station, horseshoe tossing, Nerf gun shooting range and gold mining in the sandbox.

I searched high and low to create an event that was packed with fun and not much time for standing around visiting.

My thoughts were if I keep everyone busy, they will think we are doing great, there will be no time for questions or the chance that I might break down in tears over what our family was going through.

After I worked tirelessly for weeks, Grayson asked what I was doing. It seemed I was spending our playtime doing other things. I told him I was creating the best cowboy birthday party ever, and he thought about it for a minute, nodded his head, and said, "ok." The date was getting closer, and all the supplies started piling up. Grayson again came and asked a question.

"What are we going to do with all this stuff?"
I told tell him how fun the party would be with all the games and activities. This party was going to be the most fun ever.

Then I got to work on the details. I love the details. I made denim seat cushions for the picnic table, cut handkerchief fabric into circles to cover the tops of the mason jars for their drinks, and made hand-cut letters to put on signs for EVERYTHING. Martha Stewart would have been so proud down to the very last detail. Did I mention that I am a creative person? Sometimes it shows up as crazy.

The morning of the party, I furiously ran around, giving

everyone directions and making sure everything was perfect. Grayson came up to me in his cowboy boots and overalls and said, "Momma, what do all these signs say?" I told him. Then he says, " Who did you make them all for?" I said, "You and your brother, of course."
He looks around, shuffles his feet, puts his hands on his hips and says to me,

"Momma, Grant is two, he can't read anything, and I don't think he cares that this sign tells him to dig for gold, he is just gonna throw that sand out anyway. I can't read much, and my friends don't read either. I think you did a lot of time on all this stuff for something that don't matter."

Gulp. What is that old saying? Out of the mouths of babes. I had worked so hard to make the perfect party. I had something I could sink my creative teeth into after years of being dormant. But he was right. I had spent so much time making things perfect for all our friends and family so they could see that we were doing great, and I wasn't falling apart at the seams on the inside. If I could carry out such an extravagant birthday party down to the costumes the boys wore, then that would prove that I was doing life marvelously.

Ah, but my boy. My sweet boy with such eloquent words even for five years old to call his momma out on her trying to impress the guests. Yes, it was a fabulous party that everyone talked about for years.

I thought I was doing it for my boys but was I? I was trying to prove that our life was as great as our peers, despite the heartbreak we were hiding. I had not found my footing as a mom of special needs. I hadn't found where I belonged in the scheme of this mothering thing, and I was floundering for acceptance. I disguised my pain in a pair of cowboy boots and a bedazzled, fringed blouse.

Chapter Four

Unwrap Your Gifts

I have a talent for crafting and creating things down to every last detail. There, I said it. It is a talent gifted me from God. No one else in my family has had quite the crazy ideas that have come out of my brain. I shied away from sharing that with people for years because I didn't want attention from it. I never saw it as a gift that can benefit others, or something others can enjoy. My creations seemed self-serving as something that made only me happy and relieved stress.

Our talents can also be disguised as ways to compete with the mom next door or cover up pain like the birthday party. Our gifts and talents are a part of us. God gifted them to us for specific use for his purpose. When we don't realize the gifts we have, they end up being squandered in other ways. When we are unsure of ourselves, it is easier to go with what everyone else is doing instead of embracing who we are and our own talents.

I believe we all are not living to our potential when we

don't know our gifts, talents, and strengths. When we don't know them, we can't cultivate them. Cultivating our talent takes time to find our strengths and realize our weaknesses. We can't be great at everything. Whittling away what we are not is the first step in discovering who we were created to be.

In the book of Romans, chapter 12, Paul tells us to serve God with our spiritual gifts. Even though we are all one body in Christ, we each have different functions and are unique from each other. We each have talents according to the grace given to us.

I bet you have a small idea of what your gifts may be. They may be hiding in the back of your mind, daring to show themselves on occasion. Maybe you think that it isn't your time yet, that you need to wait until your children are grown. What if your gifts overshadow your husband's? It is easy to push back your talent when it looks very different from those around you. I can't possibly be the only one who cuts fabric toppers and straw holes for mason jars from red bandannas so that toddlers can drink in a coordinated color palette.

Maybe your gifts and talents are entirely out of your comfort zone, and you fear where they might take you. Let me repeat that. You may fear where your gifts and talents might take you. I have been there too. My fear in pursuing my true passion was that I would actually succeed. *How crazy is that?*

It wasn't until I was in my forties when I began to realize my gifts and talents. I had been using them all along, but not to the extent that God had intended. Why? I didn't understand that sharing a love for nature was helping others discover it. Being a listening ear for friends who were going through hard times was a gift to them. I love to create events down to every detail. I never saw those as gifts and talents that I could use to help my family and serve my community. I believed storytelling was for bedtime, not for inspiring families out of loneliness or realizing a dream.

Knowing what your gifts and talents are is a blessing. Cultivating them builds your confidence, relieves stress, and puts you on the path that God designed for you. God gave you specific gifts to use for his glory. Be brave and find out what gift he gave just for you.

Strengths and Limitations

Let's use a school party as an example of each mom using their talents or strengths to bring an event together. Beth is gifted at organizing events, everyone says so. She can round up a cattle drive sized group of volunteers in a matter of hours. Laura makes the most amazing chocolate pie ever. She always shows up with delectable confections that you wouldn't attempt on your most confident day. However, you can't boil water, and you don't even know five people to call for a fundraiser. But you are artistic, crafty, and can turn a tin can into a colorful work of art.

It takes each of you bringing your talents and strengths to the event. Each has a part the other can't do. What would happen if you all praised each other for the skills you bring? Build each other up in the blessing you hold. Be thankful and not envious that Laura can bake, and Beth has more reach to the masses, and together, you can pull off an excellent party for the kids.

If you allow judgment, resentment, and a touch of jealousy, no matter how small, to take up room in your heart, you will not have the space to allow your talents to grow and flourish. Finding your gifts, no matter how long it takes, will set you free to follow the path you were created to take.

Finding your gifts:
- What is *one thing* that you do well?
- Do you have a gift that is helpful to others?
- Does one of your talents fill a need?
- Is there something you do that renews your spirit?

Begin with these questions to help you on your quest:

- What are your current and past hobbies?
- What activities do you enjoy?
- Do you enjoy encouraging others?
- Do you prefer a solitary activity or hobby?
- Is being social vital to you?
- Is there a handicraft you want to try?
- Do you enjoy teaching a skill?
- Are you gifted at helping others?

Chapter Five

The Utopian Society Effect

Have you ever been on an all-inclusive vacation where you never leave, and everyone is living in this bubble of food, fun, and a fantasy life? Yes, that was my honeymoon, but what happens when you step outside the resort and go home. Reality.

I think the internet can become like a Utopian society where everyone is happy and living a perfect life daily. When we turn it off, we are right back into our reality. It is not even close to all those awesome vacation photos of your college roommate and her perfect children lined up on a mountain top. You are lucky if you have had a vacation in the last five years, and at this stage of children, they would push each other off the mountain top.

Limit outside influences that can make you feel less than.....

I am talking about Pinterest, Facebook, Instagram, Twitter, and all social media outlets, including blogs. Not mine, of course. All of these can be good in specific ways and helpful. But if you have a tendency to be pulled in and then drown in their perfection, limit your time, and set boundaries. The negative feelings that these virtual worlds can bring into your life will tear at the joy in your home.

Mason Jar Madness

A few years ago, I got hooked on Pinterest. I was a latecomer to the social outlet. A friend kept sending me pins to look at and told me that Pinterest was made for me. I resisted as long as I could. I am a visual person, and the images were such a draw for me. I was mesmerized by how all these people were doing all these things I had been dreaming about! I think I stayed up until midnight for days as I explored the world of pins. Was I living a sheltered life? How did I not have twenty-five DIY projects going and photographing every step? I saw that every other homeschooling family had cute school rooms organized and color-coded, centers for every subject and extravagant supplements for every book they own. I began to dislike the space we used for school.

I wanted matching IKEA desks instead of the thrift store mismatch. If our house was bigger, I could have a geography center, science center, and five miles of bookshelves alphabetized and color-coded by genre. Accomplishing this might call for blowing out a few walls with a remodel.

Did you know that one mason jar could solve all the problems of the world? I should be using them in every room! All my life, I thought my grandmother was a spendthrift when she was really a trendsetter with all those jars. I had no idea what was going on in the world while I was living a life *without* Pinterest. Toilet paper tubes. They are the backbone of any good craft project. I began to hoard them along with mason jars until my husband informed me that I might have a problem.

I had become discontent with what I had. I wanted to live up to the pretty photos of everyone out there doing all these awesome things. I became grumpy. Grumpy at my kids because they didn't appreciate the hours I spent printing, cutting, laminating all the parts, pieces, and activities to go with Blueberries for Sal and other books. Didn't they understand that adding fifteen learning activities to every book we read was what everyone else was doing? We were missing out.

I was grumpy that my kitchen was not amazingly white with ship-lap walls, shaker cabinets, and granite counter-tops. My second-hand dining room table was not refinished in chalk paint and antiqued. It had burn marks, chipped paint, and an odd number of chairs. I bought the overpriced chalk paint, but I couldn't get the table out the back door by myself. Curtis refused to succumb to my obsession and help me paint it. The more I pinned, the more I wanted perfection. It was unrealistic.

Mutiny began to unfold in the Giles house in the form of misbehavior, sloppy chores, and missed lessons. I chose to stay home and work on projects instead of going with the family on outings. I knew this was not healthy, so on my own, I took a drastic turn. I left Pinterest for about six months.

In those six months, I realized what I already had was just what my family needed. My kitchen still functioned with twenty-year-old cabinets, and the boys didn't sit long enough to have organized desks anyway. With all the "living" we do on our beat-up dining table, painting it would be futile. Each of us has a different style, house, children, and way of life. We can't be envious of what others have and be content with our own life at the same time. I took a look around and saw all the blessings I had that didn't need painting, laminating or a complete change in lifestyle.

- How are your boundaries?
- Do you spend too much time on social media?
- Is there one platform you can let go of or limit your time?

If you need to set boundaries, what does that look like for you?

- after a certain time of day
- time limits
- specific days

Could you take a thirty-day break from social media to see what impact it makes in your life?

Chapter Six
Friendship at the Clothesline

Mona, my grandmother, shared with me that during early motherhood years, neighbors and friends came to visit several times a week. They came for coffee, yes, but there wasn't any sitting around admiring the latest DIY projects. They were folding laundry together, washing dishes, prepping supper, and building lasting relationships at the clothesline hanging diapers.

It was these friendships that saved my grandmother's sanity. As I said before, she believed her home had to be tip-top daily before she could relax. Those neighbors and friends were a lifeline for her. Can you imagine having four boys in diapers, cloth diapers at that! Mona wasn't one to air her dirty laundry of grievances with everyone. She only had a select few she regarded as close, dear friends she could trust. It was those women who were there for her in her darkest hours of motherhood.

If you are not a social butterfly, who enjoys gaggles of friends, just having one or two close friends can get you through many seasons of motherhood. You don't have to be close to every mom in the co-op or sports group. But keep your heart open. The mom you barely say hi to this year could be the woman who holds your hand during a tough season next year.

My neighbor Stephanie, who's children are close in age with mine, also decided to school her children at home for the first few years. She and I banded together as we navigated uncharted waters to find our way. It was challenging to figure out curriculum, style, support groups, co-ops, and all the failures along the way. I don't know if I would have made it without giving up if it were not for the support of Stephanie.

We felt like homeschooling outcasts many times as we tried to find where we fit in. We always had each other to fall back on. We laughed, we cried and developed an unspoken language when we were in situations that needed an exit plan. For that season in our life, we needed each other.

There have been times in motherhood that I did not have a confidant. I had acquaintances that I saw on occasion at field trips, but no one I could pour my heart out to. Prayer was the answer for me during those seasons. I prayed for strength and guidance, and I also prayed for a friend. I prayed specifically for a friend during my current season of life. It took about a year, and then the answer to my prayers was orchestrated in such a way that I knew it was only by God's design. Kristen showed up in my life right on time.

Pray for friendship.

Pray for specific needs you have for a friend.

Hold tight for the answer.

To have a good friend is one of the highest delights of life;
to be a good friend is one of the noblest
and most difficult undertakings.

Anonymous

Blinded by Appearances

Don't allow outward appearances of others or your self-doubt to rob you of a beautiful friendship. Assuming you know about someone and dismissing the opportunity will lead to loneliness and discontentment with your own life.

About six years ago, I was asked to step in last minute to teach a co-op class. I joined in on a meeting to discuss courses, and there was a mom, Elizabeth, who I had seen several times before but never really had a conversation. She was pretty, petite, and always wore the cutest clothes. Her hair was a beautiful red color, smooth, and had a cute style that just fit her. Her children were always dressed well and looked squeaky clean. Clean seems elusive in my home. Elizabeth also seemed a bit snobby because she didn't speak to me or others in the co-op unless I or someone asked her a question.

The observation of myself was as follows. I generally have one outfit that is acceptable to wear in public, I have curly hair that has its own style depending on the weather, and my boys, well dirt is attracted to all of their clothing. Clean in my boys' world is elusive.

My next thought was Wonderful; I have to work with Miss Perfect, who I am sure doesn't want to be around me because I am not even close to the type of person she would want to be friends with.

In the very first week of class, I felt pressed to go over and talk to Elizabeth. The conversation didn't go anywhere, and I felt like I may be wasting my time. However, each week, I was pressed by the Holy Spirit to go and talk to this woman. I felt like I was forcing myself on Elizabeth, who clearly was not interested in forming a friendship.

Every week for the entire semester, the Holy Spirit pressed me to talk to her. At the end of our co-op class, when everyone was saying goodbyes, I went up to Elizabeth to tell her goodbye. All of a sudden, these words came pouring out of my mouth

" Would you like to come over to my house and have coffee on the back porch while the children play?"
I was horrified that I had just done that. Surely she would say no. I knew where she lived. It was in a much more beautiful neighborhood than mine. And I was confident that she had a cleaner house than I did. Our backyard is very woodsy, and she

was not. I was sure she would say no. Elizabeth came over. It was awkward at first, then as we talked, we found more in common, and she began to open up. I started to like her. She was a lot like me.

Toward the end of our time together, she said, " Holly, I am so glad you invited us, just sitting out here is so peaceful. I needed this. I have been having some personal struggles with family this year that has taken a toll on me."

Then she said, "I have felt intimidated by you all this time because you seem to embrace homeschooling, and I have not. Thank you for showing me how alike we really are."

What! Can you believe this? This woman who I have been intimidated by all this time felt the same way about me. I spent so much time building her up in my mind as a snobby person who didn't want to be friends when she was actually distracted by heavy thoughts that were putting stress on her whole family.

Elizabeth and I became very close friends. She was the biggest cheerleader in my dreams of writing and speaking. We have prayed together during a family crisis, laughed together at field trips gone wrong, like being spit on by an Alpaca, and she has graciously volunteered in my booths at conventions.

Elizabeth showed me what a true friend could be. I taught her how to break out of a strict routine, enjoy her time with her kids, and get a little dirt on her clothes. God blessed both of us with this friendship.

God knew Elizabeth needed a friend. She needed a friend that was different than her. A friend with a fresh perspective on struggles with motherhood and homeschooling. If I had resisted His call to me to press on and keep pushing for friendship, we both would have lost out. I can be quick to pass on getting to know people. I have been burned more times than I can count. It is safer for me to stay in my bubble with my boys. However, God does know our hearts and what we need.

Elizabeth and I forged a friendship along with a few other moms and had several years of good times with our kids. We have all moved on, and we run in different circles now. Elizabeth and I don't get to see each other quite as often. We were on the phone last fall trying to find time to get together, but so many things prevented it. Schooling, housework, and obligations kept us from catching up.

Our discussion turned to freezer cooking and meal planning. We both had wanted to create better meal schedules and try freezer cooking but had not done it yet. Then we thought, why don't we do it together?

Freezer, Fun, and Coffee

We picked four meals. We decided to make four of each meal to test the recipe. We split the ingredients, and we met at Elizabeth's house. In two hours, we cooked, laughed, and caught up on the latest news.

> *We fed our souls with friendship while preparing*
> *meals to feed our family.*

We decided it was much more fun to do that together. It was a good use of our limited time, our children could play, and we left with eight meals for our freezer.

The season of friendship in your life:

- One or two close friends can get you through many seasons of motherhood. List the women in your life from the ones closest to acquaintances.

- Is there one particular person that you have felt pressed to speak with, but haven't?

Comparisons will lead to loneliness and discontentment with your own life. Being happy with what you have comes from your faith in God and the blessings he has given you, not someone else.

- What are the areas that you struggle with in comparison?

- List them and challenge yourself to pray over them daily.

I struggle with a small house. In the past, I have spent wasted hours sitting in my friends' big beautiful homes, wishing. When my discontentment was wedging into my marriage, I began to pray, and that is when God showed me how my small house, back porch, and pond were a refuge for others. I used not to want to invite moms over for coffee because my place is little, old, and dirt is generally our floor covering from tracking it in.

But the reality is just like Elizabeth; they look beyond all of that and relax. I now realize my blessing of a small house, and the woodsy yard is a way to serve. Serve friends with tranquility, simplicity, and calm. Their kids may leave dirtier than they have ever been, but it's worth it.

Are you involved in a regular group, homeschooling support group, park day, book club, or other activity to meet new people?

- Make an effort to introduce yourself to several people each time. Even if you are an introvert.
- Don't assume all the other moms know each other and are not new like you.
- Keep making an effort. Every time you speak to at least one person and the people who seem to be in charge if it is an organized group.

Hello, I'm over here in the back row.

I am an introvert by nature. Yes, I do get up and speak to hundreds of people as part of my job, and I love it. But it is not the same as being alone in a crowd of peers and not knowing anyone. I have given up way too soon on several groups because I felt like no one talked to me, made me feel welcome, or I felt like I didn't fit in. I felt sorry for myself. I was a lonely homeschooling mom. I had one great friend who homeschooled, but we both wanted more friends.

I went to one homeschooling group that had support meetings open to the public once a month. They usually had great speakers, and I was always encouraged. I would smile at people as I came in and sit in the back. I hung around briefly after to see if any of the leaders would come to speak to me. Some might say hi but mostly were engaged in other conversations. So, I gave up. I would go to meetings when I could, and I saw many of the same women at different functions, but I resigned that I would not make friends. I just didn't fit in.

A few years later, I received a call from one of those moms who was on the board of this homeschooling organization. She said they were looking for a new Vice President and wanted to take the group in new directions, and my name came up. She said they all thought I would be a great fit in helping moms in the group and new moms coming in. I was shocked. Me? I talked with my husband, and we discussed the duties. I had this feeling like I could make a change in people feeling lonely when they came to those group meetings. I would not make people feel like they didn't belong. I would make everyone feel part of the group.

Mama Lessons

You know how God puts you on paths that you think are to make a difference for other people, but it was really to show you the way and change your way of thinking? Yep, that is what this was. The title of Vice President was actually a front to showing me the heart of all those moms who I thought were in their own clicks and not welcoming to others. The truth was, they were just like me. They were trying to get through the day with school, activities, tantrums, and dinner. Showing up to serve others was in their heart, but sometimes it took all they had to get there.

I began to understand that just because I was the newbie somewhere didn't mean I should expect others to make all the effort to bring me into the fold. I had to give as good as I expected to get. I had to step out of my comfort zone and approach others, be approachable, and realize I am not the only one stressing out over what may be going on in my house while I am out for the evening.

As I listened and watched more carefully to the women around me, I learned that many of them in leadership positions were going through their own issues with marital separation, troubled children, job loss, or health decline with family members. I had not considered that the women in charge or leading events actually had real world problems like the rest of us.

In changing my attitude about "fitting in" I found new friendships and shared issues that allowed comfort to one another.

Let God open your heart and your eyes to opportunities that may be disguised as mommy cliques or places you don't seem to fit in. When fear and self-doubt creep in, it can steal the joy you were meant to find.

Chapter Seven
Where Did All The Cookies Go?

Let's talk a little bit about food. If you have taken on the suburban homestead movement and are growing some of your own food, raising chickens, and are striving to be an all organic mama, that is awesome. I think that is amazing, and I applaud your effort for your family. I have a friend Christine who has turned her yard, front, and back into a garden. Her family eats from it all year long. She has three chickens in the for eggs and composting. She loves to help friends start their own garden and forage for the rest. I admire her spirit and love of growing her food.

I come from generations of farmers who grew what they ate. I believed I had that same spirit until year after year; the pitiful bounty my gardening produced forced my husband to tell me to stop. He said it cost us more money than if I bought it all at the store. I still dabble here and there because I will give up! However, the bottomless pits that are my sons force me to buy large quantities of food from any source available on my budget.

We do raise chickens. We are down to two girls now that give me more enjoyment for my soul than eggs for my table. Although when they do lay, the eggs taste amazing. If we are talking cost and budgeting, the hens cost us more than buying eggs, but to our family and the life lessons we have learned in eight years raising chickens, it is worth it.

If you are a mama who throws white bread and Lucky Charms in your grocery cart to fill the gaps of hunger in your kids, you are just as awesome as any other mom. My cousin grew up on Corn Pops cereal and bologna sandwiches on wonder bread. She is beautiful, healthy, and makes better food choices for her children. Don't be intimidated by other people's food choices and do the best you can. My philosophy is when you know better, you do better. I buy or make the best possible food choices for my family. However, you will find pre-made, ready-to-serve meals in my freezer and pantry because, in the end, I need to feed my family on my budget and fill up teenagers too.

Many factors play into a family's food budget. Some may not have consistent income, and others may grow some of their food, be subsidized in some way, or share food sources.

My mom and stepdad Randy live next door. Randy is an incredible cook who loves to experiment frequently. He sends dinner over at least once a week and their leftovers too. What a blessing for us to help stretch our already tight food bill.

My son Grayson is a hunter. He keeps our freezer full of meat that we use all year. I don't buy meat very often. This allows me to buy more vegetables and fruit that would sometimes be too expensive for me to afford with my budget. These two food factors are not information most people would know about our family but plays a significant role in how food is provided for us.

I see many posts in online groups asking about food budgets, and the responses run wild. Again, do not compare your circumstances on a fraction of the information. For instance, Lisa posted online; she only spends $150 a month on groceries for her family of six. Melissa read that and was brought to tears because she is trying to hold steady at $850 a month for her family of four.

Location, income, circumstances, and many more sources are a tremendous factor in each family's ability to put food on the table. There can not be a comparison.

On the other hand, don't judge people's food choices, either healthy or unhealthy. You never know what season of life that person is living. In the past, I have had to be very strict with my youngest son's ingredients due to allergies and other issues. For a time, I went way overboard. I have been accused of ruining my oldest son's life because he did not have a Twinkie until he was fifteen when his aunt gave him one.

It can be hard and time-consuming to make most everything from scratch and keep up that pace. It is also hard to tell your son he can't have the gooey green cupcakes all the other kids are having at a birthday party. Those moments run deep in a child's memory. Choose your food battles wisely when their health is not in danger.

Next Generation Biscuits

Do you cook with your children? If you don't, start now. No matter what age they are they can begin destroying, I mean dusting your kitchen one cup of flour at a time. Yes, you will have to let go of perfection and a perfectly clean kitchen, for about twenty years. But it is so worth it. Children love to cook, and presenting their parents with a concoction of their own is a look of joy you don't want to miss.

Mona, my grandmother, taught my oldest Grayson how to make her famous buttermilk biscuits. I have never been able to perfect her biscuits. Each time they were always baseballs, but Grayson has the knack. They are the best biscuits you have ever put in your mouth, seriously. However, when he is done, there is flour all over the counter, the stove, the cabinet doors, and the refrigerator. There is even flour *inside* the refrigerator. I don't know how on earth he does it. Yet the look on his face when he presents his breakfast to the family is worth it. He also makes the best-scrambled eggs ever.

As he has gotten older, he has become better about learning to clean up after himself. It is a skill that has taken years for him to grasp and fully be aware of his far-reaching mess. Teaching him to cook from a young age has been a blessing because he is now, at sixteen, capable of preparing a meal for the family that can take the burden off of me when days are super busy.

Where Did All The Cookies Go?

Cooking has been a part of our home education from the beginning. Anytime I could have them in the kitchen cooking, was a time I could instill in them what they need to know in the future to live on their own. Both boys are handy in the kitchen and are not afraid to dig in and whip up a meal or a mean plate of brownies. Life skills are at the top of my list in child-rearing. They are the key to a good foundation for the future.

The kitchen is the pride and joy of many women. Handing over the reins to kids is like running fingernails on a chalkboard. It is challenging to bring children into the kitchen and enjoy your time with them. I am asking you to take a deep breath and use those moments to build confidence and a lifelong relationship with your children.

I have heard from many people, men, women, myself included, who did not learn to cook because no one wanted their kitchens messy or to take the extra time involved to teach along the way. I read a recent article where eighty percent of the people polled between the ages of 18 – 26 did not have basic cooking skills. Many cited that growing up, their home lives were busy, and mom just wanted to get a meal on the table. The thought to teach along the way was not considered.

Cooking does take a bit of skill. Simple meals are possible for young children to make.

What can you do?

- Make a list of 5 simple meals you already cook for your family.

- Set aside specific time weekly or monthly to have your children make those meals with you.

- Make a family cookbook together of favorite meals.

- Have kids night where the children do all the cooking.

- Rotate breakfast, lunch, and dinner meals between children.

- Have fun with your kids. Don't get upset with the mess.

Chapter Eight
Wash, Dry, Fold, and Repeat

I grew up in a single-parent household. I was an only child, and my mom had to work several jobs to keep a roof over our heads and food on the table. By the time I was eight years old, I was a latch key kid. I fixed my own meals, washed clothes, and did a lot of the housework. When I got married, I dreamed of children of my own. I knew that I did not want them to have to do tons of chores. I wanted them to feel loved by taking care of all their needs. I wanted to show love by serving them.

That idea works when they are babies and very young but the reality is learning to do chores from a young age is serving them. I don't think they need to do *all* the housework, of course, and starting with one or two and working up as they grow is the best way to instill the importance of learning those skills.

It takes years for children to master skills necessary to complete chores that they will need when they grow up, become adults and have a household of their own. I know it is so much easier to do the chores ourselves and less time consuming. You may like towels folded a certain way or t-shirts done in thirds to fit in the drawer. Lower your standards to meet them where they are now. Helping them improve over time is what we need to do in raising kids who actually know how to do things.

When life gets busy, and the couch is covered in laundry, and the to-do list is a mile long, it can be mind-numbing to put the brakes on progress to help a child do a chore that seems to take forever. Of course, there will be days like this, and getting it done and out of the way may be what needs to happen. My boys do a great deal of the housework with me each week. Is our house spotless? No, far from it, but I am spending these years training them consistently in jobs they don't care about now, but one day it will click. I don't think cleaning toilets is any more fun at ten years old than it is fifty years old.

When I ask Grant to clean the living room windows outside, I know there will be so many streaks it will make the windows look dirtier than they were before. Some days I point it out, others I do not. The work my boys do is acceptable for their age and ability level. However, if we have company, I will be in the bathroom doing a once-over for sure.

Getting it done

I do not have any magical chore charts or incentives that will make your children gleefully do their chores. I have tried at least ten different charts over the years. I have painted, cut, laminated, and sorted chore sticks until I realized that all the fancy, colorful charts were really for my benefit and not theirs. They still see the same chores no matter how gussied up they are. Now I have a simple daily printed sheet for each boy with the day's assignments of household duties. I have a master file on my computer so I can change responsibilities or add to them. I print them out on Sunday evening and post with a magnet on the refrigerator each day. They mark through them when they are complete.

Please don't think I have dutiful children who wait anxiously for their chart to be posted each day — quite the opposite. If I did not tell them each and every day to look at the chart, which is displayed in the same spot every day, they would never even look at it and revel in the filth.

Start young and choose according to age appropriateness. Decide what season you are in, and let go of some of the reins to keep your sanity. Laundry can put me in a depression quick because it multiplies all over my furniture so fast I can't keep up. I know that I cannot do it alone. I have two boys who are quite capable of handling this job for me. Now, when I say put it away, they might not have understood that that meant inside the drawers so they can shut. However, some days, I am just happy to be able to sit on the couch that I don't care how it got into their room or where it landed.

Having responsibilities from a young age makes children feel like a part of something greater than themselves. They want boundaries and jobs. It helps them feel a sense of belonging to the family and that they have a purpose that matters and makes a difference to the greater of the family.

Chapter Nine

A Marriage Hung Out to Dry

Let the wife make the husband glad to come home, and let him make her sorry to see him leave. - *Martin Luther*

As I said in chapter one, my husband Curtis and I had no idea what we were getting ourselves into when we said "I do" in our early twenties. As I suppose most young newlyweds do not. We have had some struggles along the way that would put any marriage to the test. The stresses we faced in the first few years, dealing with infertility, and then a special needs child put a strain on our marriage. It got to the point that I felt like we were living separate lives but living in the same house. All of Curtis' faults were magnified, and that is all I could see. I had lost sight of the man I thought I married.

Deep in the daily grind of a toddler, tantrums, doctors' appointments, and lack of sleep, I reached a point where I believed that ending our marriage would be the best solution. I never wanted that for my children since I grew up in a broken home myself. Yet I was miserable. I felt that I had given everything to this marriage, and I was being ignored, unappreciated, and exhausted from what our life had become. In my mind there was no other way out of the misery playing in my head.

I began to pray about the situation. I began to pray for Curtis. I prayed that God would make him a better husband, to show him how I was drowning, and to change him into the man I needed. I was the one that did everything for our family at times, giving more than I had to get through the days. I began to journal about my feelings, and then slowly, several books came across my path that I began to read. Over time, Curtis did not change, but I did.

God began showing me my faults and thoughts that were the root of some of our issues. At first, I got a little upset. I was praying for God to fix Curtis and instead He dared to show me my own faults. I believed I was the perfect wife giving everything in this marriage, why did I have to change?

Over the next year, God made me face the truth about how my upbringing as an only child in a broken home, with sometimes unusual family dynamics, had shaped my thoughts on men, marriage, and relationships. It affected our relationship from the beginning and the way Curtis reacted, or didn't react, set a path in our marriage, that over the years, landed us in a position of unhappiness.

During this time as I read, prayed and journaled, God broke me down, molded me and shaped me into a better wife and mother by making me take a hard look at my contribution to our marriage. It was difficult for me when I truly realized that maybe I was not the perfect wife I thought I was. I was never taught to love and appreciate men. The role models in my life struggled with their own demons that prevented them from seeing a little girl who was learning from them. I grew up watching Disney movies that filled my imagination with Cinderella and Prince Charming and that fairy tales do come true. I was unaware that real love takes work, sacrifice, and submission.

As the year went on with my revelations, some I shared

with Curtis and others I did not. I noticed a change in the atmosphere of our home. As I gave a little, so did Curtis. It may not have been noticeable to an onlooker into our life, but it was to me. We both knew that if we could still be standing together after all we had been through, we are worth a little more effort and less ego.

When I decided to hand myself and my marriage over to God honestly, he transformed it. Communication, misconceptions, and false ideals of each other played a significant role in chipping away at a marriage that God had put together for his purpose. If you are struggling in your marriage, give it over to God. Let go of your hurt feelings, your list of who does what, and who doesn't (this takes strength). God can restore your marriage with time and patience. Being able to look within and admitting your own mistakes can help you along the journey, even if your husband does not. Your faith in restoration can be strong enough for the both of you. If you get weary, hit your knees. Ask for strength to see it through.

Our marriage is far from perfect. Perfection is not attainable; living life together is. We still have hard seasons, and of course, there are days I want to push him out the door.

Those are moments in time and possibly hormonal. Moments that if I don't take a step back and breathe can turn into regrettable words.

For me, what has changed the most is that at the end of the day, I can look at Curtis and say I love you for who you are and not who *I want* you to be.

On the other hand, if your marriage has turned to separation or divorce, do not shut out your friends or resources within your community. As women, we tend to be close-lipped about what is going on. How can we say anything to the moms in the co-op with happy marriages? There is no judgment in friendship. You need a sounding board, or a mom who can take your kids while you take a breath, or a resource to help you take steps toward your future.

Prayer can bring you the person you need in this season of life.

Chapter Ten
The Caretaker of the Clothespins

Are you taking a little time for yourself every day? Every week? How about once a month? I don't mean a spa retreat. I mean a silent cup of coffee, reading God's word, and reflecting on your week, year, your dreams, and goals. Read a book for sheer pleasure and not for your children. Curious George doesn't count.

Those seven years that our lives were wrapped up in making Grayson whole with doctors' appointments, therapies, and countless sleepless nights, I just forgot about me. I compared it to keeping all the clothespins on the line. I had to be diligent that they all stay on the line, don't drop any and keep the line moving with the next load.

I didn't think I deserved to do anything for myself or by myself. A nice cup of coffee alone at the local coffee shop, no way. Selfish.

I thought I was not a good mother by doing something I loved or just sit quietly without talking to anyone. When I began to come out of that period, I was lost. My identity had become "the constant caretaker." I looked in the mirror and saw someone I didn't recognize, and it felt like I was coming out of a fog and didn't know who I was or where I belonged. Have you ever felt like that?

I was a bit depressed, and I knew that I needed to do something about it. First, I decided to work on a sewing project that I had put up in the closet years earlier. I had such a peaceful feeling each night after the boys were asleep working on it. I loved it.

Next, I decided that I would do something creative with all of those mason jars I had been collecting in the garage(Pinterest). I wanted to make a chandelier for our back porch and string lights to hang from the canopy. It took about a week to complete with trial and error and help from the boys.

Along the way, Curtis noticed I was not as snappy as usual, and a smile had taken its place. He reminded me of how crafting makes me happy and that I needed to have a project now and then to have time for myself. The boys even noticed a difference when I took a break for myself. Carve out time for yourself. Whatever that looks like in your home.

- Take small bits of time.

Is there a hobby or activity that feeds your soul?

- Give it your time at least once a week.
- Communicate your personal needs with your spouse to make it happen.

We are not designed to be superwoman. I don't believe we really want to be anyway. Somehow we have convinced ourselves that we are not enough if we can't do it all and we sacrifice ourselves in the process. God tells us to rest. We need a spiritual rest to be a good wife and mother.

If we give everything away for the sake of measuring up to the world's standards, we are doing our children a disservice. We need to refresh ourselves to be able to give them what they need. To have the presence of mind to train, nurture and love.

I encourage you to journal during every season of motherhood. How you journal will change with your time frame and mindset. I have been journaling off and on for over twenty years, and it has made a difference in the paths I take. Some of my journals were daily, weekly, monthly, and a few had almost yearly entries. However, when I look back, especially during difficult times, I see how God has been leading me and answering prayers. Journaling can be an encouragement to realize God's presence in your life and that He has been with you all the time. Without my journals, I may not have seen the pattern to inspire me to keep going. It can be so easy to forget when we are in the trenches of tantrums and forgotten dreams.

I do caution you to be careful with "self-care". This trending movement does have merit in that we can't run ourselves to the point of exhaustion; however, anytime "self" is the main focus, it can run off in the ditch.

In Colossians 2:8 it speaks of not letting anyone or thing take you captive. Self-care can become an attractive captivator of our time. Don't let yourself be lured into too many self-care activities that cause problems with your time and duty at home.

Chapter Eleven

The Beauty Within the Clothesline

"Together, my wife and I are building the kingdom of God, exercising dominion, beating back the weeds of stinky diapers, tending the garden God has put us in. This is why my dear wife vacuums the floor, for it is part of the garden she has been called to dress and to keep. But she is doing this not as raw duty, but because she understands that she is exercising dominion over the dust, for the glory of Christ." *R.C. Sproul*

We have talked together about significant points that can help us to enjoy the seasons we encounter in our lives. Let's recap with some questions for you to ponder and then write out your answers. Give yourself a timeline to work on them and accomplish your goals. I do not have a formula for figuring it all out. I have learned to reduce everything down to the bare basics and then work back up from there. Then, add back in what is necessary in each season.

Find the Beauty in Your Days

What are the three most important things to you, in this season, that you want to accomplish with your children consistently? It could be daily, weekly, monthly, depending on your answer.

-
-
-

What are three areas or specific chores that you need to be accomplished every day to survive?

-
-
-

List three simple personal goals you want to achieve, practice, or put into place.

-
-
-

List three simple goals for your marriage that can be accomplished in one month.

-
-
-

What is preventing you from moving from surviving to thriving in your life right now?

-

My answer? Myself. Truly allowing what I know to be true

to take hold and stick. I know that God has a specific plan for my children, myself, and my husband. I know that building lasting family relationships and guiding my family toward the Savior is my number one goal. That is my bare-bones fundamental life goal. However, working up from there into a rhythm that works gets distorted when I allow influences, old habits, and the thoughts that I am not good enough, to cloud my judgment on what I know is right for my family.

I believe that when we take on too much as a family, the roots get washed away quickly. If we divide our time into too many sections, there is no way to bring them back together again. Mega multitasking is what I call it. Some families call their routine divide and conquer to get through the day.

The enemy loves that term, divide and conquer, because that is just what it does if we are not careful with our time. The fundamentals of family are under attack in our world. Keep your eye on your clothesline mamas. You are the first line of defense.

After years of on-the-go, we have now chosen a very simple routine and way of life. We spend the majority of our time together in all aspects of life. This is our time to build character and lasting bonds that will carry our children on to the greatness God has planned. Why would I want to give it up for outward things?

"Just Sit"
Laura Ingalls Wilder

Multitasking takes away the joy that can be found in
the simplest of tasks. It can create a mindset that idleness
is bad. It is in that idleness that we see the beauty of our lives.
The funny moments, kids laughter, a milestone,
a look that translates our love for one another.

Chapter Twelve

Fear in the Hole

Our home is filled with mischief and mayhem weekly. This particular day is one of many where God has brought me to my knees and back to what I know is right. He is faithful. He's got my back if I will allow him.

Tuesday morning started way off track, and I was pretty frazzled by 9 am. The boys seemed to wake up cranky, and that never gets our lessons started well. I was in the kitchen with Grant 6, washing grapes as Grayson 9, came in the back door from chicken duty. He had tracked mud from the back door, through the living room, and into the bathroom. At least I hoped it was mud.

As I got the broom out, I looked up to see Grant grab the sink sprayer. I didn't think he knew how to use it, so I quickly got to the sink just in time for him to say,

"Mommy, how do you use this?". At the same time, pressing down on the button and pointed it at the ceiling. When the water shot up and hit the ceiling, it scared him half to death, and he then turned the nozzle on me. I got a good soaking in the face before I got it out of his hands.

As the water dripped off the ceiling, poor Grant had a terrified look on his face. I told him it would be fine if he would help me clean it up. As I am up on the step ladder wiping down the ceiling, I hear Grayson calling from the bathroom, "the toilet is clogged again!". Great, I thought. "And why is there brown stuff coming up in the shower?" Oh, no. We had been babying our septic tank for years, and it was on its last leg or flush. At that point, I just wanted to call it quits for the day and get in the car and leave.

I told the boys to go outside and play while I cleaned everything up and tried to collect myself and find my coffee. Grant asked if he could dig a hole. I said, "sure!" Digging holes was his favorite past time. I began to clean up the mess in the bathroom and kitchen. After a while, Grayson came in upset and telling me that Grant was stuck in a hole. "What do you mean, stuck in a hole?" I said.

"Mom, Grant is literally stuck in a hole, and I can't get him out, I tried to pull him out but I can't, you have to come!" Well, I thought that sounded crazy, possibly a rouse to finish me off by pushing me into a hole, so I wasn't too concerned about it or in a hurry. I took my time getting on my shoes and walked out back to find Grant, knee's first, down in a narrow hole, stuck. Miffed at the situation that pulled me away from septic slime, I walked over, grabbed his arm, and yanked in a not-so-loving way. Nothing. Huh. I grabbed both arms and pulled again. Nothing, not even a grain of sand moved.

I asked, "Grant, how on earth did this happen?" He replied, "Momma, I was digging and digging, and then I got tired. I just wanted to rest, so I sat down on my knees and then started to slide into the hole, and now I am stuck, please get me out!"

I pondered the situation and reached for my phone that was in my back pocket. I was going to call my husband Curtis but realized he was out of town for work. He is rarely out of town for work. I thought of my mother, who lived next door and remembered she was out of the area for the day. I called my neighbor down the street, who also home-schools, and she was gone for the day on a field trip.

I began to feel a little uneasy because the thought had crossed my mind that I might actually have to call the fire department. After a few neighborly knocks, I discovered no one was home on our street.

Grayson was very nervous, which translated to excited behavior. He said, "Momma, you have to call the fire department, Grant will be stuck forever if we don't. There is no one else to help us; what are we gonna do?"

I replied, "Now let's just settle down and think about this for a minute. I really don't want to call the fire department. We live in a small town, and here we are, it's 10 am on a Tuesday morning. There are two school-age boys digging holes in a backyard in their pajamas. Then, there is the possibility that they may or may not see seven chickens running around in our backyard yard that we technically are not supposed to have in our town. There has to be another alternative."

I exhausted my list of people to call and began to become anxious myself. There was no one home on my street, which was very unusual, and I wasn't quite sure what to do next. Grant began to panic as his legs were starting to hurt; he was scared.

His panic made me panic, which made him panic more, and then my panic turned to fear. Grayson got more excited, and his usual can-do spirit was fleeting. This funny incident was quickly turning into a serious situation. Tears ran down Grant's face as he pleaded with me to get him out. I decided to call 911.

As I reached for my phone all of a sudden, my fear turned into a presence of calm. I said to the boys, "Let's pray." Grayson and I stood over Grant, holding hands, and I prayed. I asked Jesus to please help us out of this situation. To take care of Grant and let him be unharmed by the pressure of the sand. I asked him to help me think clearly and not out of fear. I didn't know what to do. I needed His help.

As we let go of our hands, my phone began to ring. It was my neighbor Stephanie who was away on a field trip. She said that her husband just called, he forgot a tool he needed for work, and he was on his way home. He would be at my house in five minutes.

Dan was like a knight in shining armor as he came in the back gate. He laughed when he saw Grant and settled him down with a few jokes about the situation. Dan is a large truck mechanic, a big guy, and with a little work, and some time, it took both of us to get Grant out of that hole. What a relief I felt.

As we stood there shaking off all the emotions of the last two hours, I realized what had just happened. You see, God knew our need before it happened that morning. He knew I had become a frazzled mother who was riddled with anxiety that our day had gotten off track from school. He knew I tried to handle the house disasters alone and was thinking of calling it quits. He also knew I was working from a place of fear.

Dan worked forty-five minutes away. The plan was already set in motion earlier that morning when he left without that tool that he needs every day.

God was just waiting for me to give my control over to Him.

He was waiting for me to ask for His help.

Motherhood can put us in the seat of wanting to control everything. If we didn't do it, who would right? Being in control of all that we face as wives, mothers, and those that home-school can be exhausting. In that exhaustion, confusion and fear can take over. It can cause panic and rash decisions that can take our day, week, or year in an undesirable direction. However, when we lay it out, everything before the Lord, He has it under control.

> Prayer can be the key when you are ready to hang motherhood on the clothesline.

To dig deeper into the questions and bible text discussed in this book, purchase the accompanying journal.

Hanging Motherhood On the Clothesline JOURNAL

Acknowledgments

This book went to publish the week before my forty-ninth birthday. It was a moment that brought tears and the big ugly cry for me. It was the culmination of a year that I spent discovering the gifts and talents I had long forgotten.

In His infinite ways and with a sense of humor, God brought me full circle and performed the smallest miracles that brought a year full of change for the better, and a spit-shine to the rose-colored glasses I had been wearing. Thank you Jesus for forty-eight years of grace!

I thank my soul-sister Mary Beth who never lets me feel sorry for myself. She walks beside on hard days even from four states away, always believes in my crazy ideas, and cheers the loudest through trials and always knows where I'm going before I do. Roadschool Moms rock!

I was blessed to have grandmothers who imparted their wisdom in unconventional ways that shaped who I became as a mother. Both of them would be tickled to see their photos on the back cover, maybe. Granny's parting advice is to never leave the house without lipstick. Meemee would tell you that if you touch just one person's life for the better it has been a life well lived.

I dedicate this to them. I can't wait until one fine morning when we all will meet on God's celestial shores and I get to hug them again. Oh, Glory Hallelujah, by and by, I'll fly away! I love you Granny and Meemee.

Holly M. Giles inspires families with her books, down-to-earth motivational talks across the country, blog and podcast. Holly has a passion for families. Through sharing her experiences, she touches the heart and makes you feel like you are not alone.

Holly is a Florida Master Naturalist, and author of three unit-study style curriculum books focusing on nature and community. She lives with her husband and two children in their own old Florida paradise. Together they lead a simple life among the chaos that raising boys brings. As a family they enjoy exploring history and nature at state and local parks, and along roads less traveled.

Most days you will find Holly sitting out on her back porch watching the wildlife, meaning her boys or the birds, or talking to a friend, and being grateful for every moment she gets to spend at her little house on the lake.

Connect with Holly and her latest adventures online at https://www.thegilesfrontier.com

Or email her at holly@thegilesfrontier.com

www.ingramcontent.com/pod-product-compliance
Lightning Source LLC
Chambersburg PA
CBHW051347040426
42453CB00007B/455